SOLVE *for* DESIRE

SOLVE *for* DESIRE

poems by

CAITLIN BAILEY

Lindquist & Vennum Prize for Poetry * *Selected by Srikanth Reddy*

MILKWEED EDITIONS

Published 2017 by Milkweed Editions
Printed in the United States of America
Cover design by Mary Austin Speaker
Cover illustration by Andrea Amadio, from the *Codice Roccobonella*, ca. 1445
Author photo by Lucas Botz
17 18 19 20 21 5 4 3 2 1
First Edition

Milkweed Editions, an independent nonprofit publisher, gratefully acknowledges sus-
taining support from the Jerome Foundation; the Lindquist & Vennum Foundation; the
McKnight Foundation; the National Endowment for the Arts; the Target Foundation;
and other generous contributions from foundations, corporations, and individuals.
Also, this activity is made possible by the voters of Minnesota through a Minnesota
State Arts Board Operating Support grant, thanks to a legislative appropriation from
the arts and cultural heritage fund, and a grant from Wells Fargo. For a full listing of
Milkweed Editions supporters, please visit milkweed.org.

Library of Congress Cataloging-in-Publication Data

Names: Bailey, Caitlin, author.
Title: Solve for desire : poems / Caitlin Bailey.
Description: First edition. | Minneapolis, Minnesota : Milkweed Editions,
   [2017] |
Identifiers: LCCN 2017028617 (print) | LCCN 2017032354 (ebook) | ISBN
   9781571319753 (ebook) | ISBN 9781571314994 (softcover : acid-free paper)
Classification: LCC PS3602.A533 (ebook) | LCC PS3602.A533 A6 2017 (print) |
   DDC 811/.6--dc23
LC record available at https://lccn.loc.gov/2017028617

Milkweed Editions is committed to ecological stewardship. We strive to align our book
production practices with this principle, and to reduce the impact of our operations in
the environment. We are a member of the Green Press Initiative, a nonprofit coalition
of publishers, manufacturers, and authors working to protect the world's endangered
forests and conserve natural resources. *Solve for Desire* was printed on acid-free 100%
postconsumer-waste paper by Thomson-Shore.

For Grete

Contents

Finding you everywhere   nowhere I travel
in this spaciousness are you absent.

DEBORAH KEENAN

Georg Trakl was an Austrian poet born in 1887. He was addicted to drugs for much of his life and had an extremely close relationship with his younger sister, Grete, the extent of which nobody knows. Grete was a gifted pianist and also addicted to drugs. Georg trained as a pharmacist in Vienna and began to publish his poetry. Grete, meanwhile, lived in Vienna and Berlin, studying piano. Georg eventually enlisted in the army and completed several tours before serving as a pharmacist and medic during World War I. After a horrific incident in Gródek (in modern-day Ukraine) in 1914, wherein he attempted suicide, Georg was hospitalized in Poland and ultimately died following what might have been a purposeful cocaine overdose—perhaps because of the atrocities of war he witnessed. He left all of his money and belongings to Grete. Grete committed suicide at a party less than three years later.

I.

Whoever Drinks from Me

Come, let us go away together into the wide world.
—THE BROTHERS GRIMM

Be not tiger nor wolf to rend me,
    but brother as deer.
Brother as thirst.
Quarrel of forest, windfall of firs.
Water meant to wound
    we repurpose.

Too dangerous to keep you
    in the world.

Take to the woods, deer brother.
    Dear brother.
    Here I adorn you.
    Adore you.

Here is our sorrow tree.
    Here is our hollow.
        Here only the sweetest grass.
O, your crown of rushes.

Finally our good hour.
Our gold all-encompassing.
    I will never, never leave you.

Deer brother. Dear brother.

Lost Letter

This is the first time I've written to you,
and I know now why they called me *little witch*.
My hands have done terrible things.
I remember the first time, your hand cupped
over the glass and over mine, O charging desire—
the welcome rush of the wild heart, poppies
blooming under my skin, a perfect red burst.
And now he's in the other room, and I can't
be long remembering you. You wore your anger
like a bare coat until I plucked myself from your
pocket.   I knew nothing of loss.

PIGEONS

Once we walked into a field and watched pigeons
black out the sky, thousands of wings whirring,

and it was a wonder they stayed aloft.
The most brilliant part of you exists to haunt me:

a bomb in the womb or men in the rafters.
Sometimes I can't believe my heart,

how it continues.
How it isn't black and withered,

how the chambers remain clear,
the beat plain and perfect.

CHURCH, HIPBONE

Ready tender mass. Glossy rope, we bare our teeth.
Equal the church, the hipbone, the sliced ocean.
That old yank in the throat, bedded for days. Perpetual tangle.
Something bent, fashioned in fits, memory of your arm
filling a sleeve. A blue whale's heart is the size of a small car
and I am finding it hard to imagine anyone who would not
be moved to think of that vehicle. I want to drive fast
into your mouth, leave nothing on the table. Ridge inside
of me, hurt spot continually worried, thumb brushed
against collarbone until it begins to crumble. Which parts
belong to me? Just the blossoming, or the tongued flat skin?
Relief when you appear. If I were fastened to any question:
hands laced together.

This Is the House

Desire fogs through the halls. We build
the house with cedar strappings. The salt
disaster of our skin whirls through doorways.
The rooms are smug, spotted. We find chips
of paint in the sheets, rub our backs raw.
Grease the floor with salve, slip from room
to room. Worry the edges of our gowns
and wear them tattered. Smartly, I kiss
the soles of your feet. We bury our luck
in the firmest piece of land.

Poem about Desire

spun sugar and roasted chestnuts
glass and stones

something about refracted light,
my split allegiance

Prater, Riesenrad
that ring against the sky

The Heart Is to a Pleasant Thing

Compare the heart to any pleasant thing.

Compare an apple to a snake.

Failed experiments we are bound to apply endlessly.

Or ignore entirely.

In any case, we are rarely seated simply.

Here is the tool I currently find useful.

Snake's middle, or some callous bulge in the peel.

I intended to love only what was given.

It's difficult to find the wound.

To walk into a field and obscure anything.

To leave each flower picked clean.

Historically, the last petal becomes your fortune.

He loves me not.

Everything is made equal by darkness.

Let's see how the trees can rebound.

Let's see how I can make you mine.

DETONATE

There were always things to tell you.

The way it would be if we buttoned
any particular button. How I would
spend the year holding back a sneeze.
How the orange puckered
in the drawer, a shriveled bomb.

We wanted everything:
bodies gabled or bent over with joy.

It was easy to forget the wires
geometried through the house.
The dark powder along the baseboards.
I looked ahead and
saw only

you: bright suture in a lined palm.

INCANTARE

In another universe there is a room
where we sleep like planks.

Sawdust drifts from the bedding,
an apple in the mouth of the wounded.

There are nine parts to this story,
and a snake that takes its time with my throat.

Sinew to sinew is penance for wreckage.
For illicit tincture.

Bone to bone is how I say *let me live
in your mouth. Let me sleep in your knee socket.*

I am trying to pin something intangible
to my shirtsleeves.

The amulet could be anything.
It's not a sign of my lessening.

Someone has replaced your heart with raw meat.
That delicacy. I'm working on a trick

where I come across sated.
Where I don't remember how to be ravenous.

Poem about Desire

If a horse is allowed
to graze freely after a winter
in the barn
it becomes sick with pleasure.

Right Light

Bring me to the lip of the evening again, again;
palm my best parts. If we're lucky, rain. You like talking
your way inside me, swelling the dark with spondee.
I am split air, tessellated sky. Tell me how it used to be.
Let me gorge myself even on truth, your crooked verbs.
Words forever the best meal, gorgeous mash of syllables.
Here our bodies lead secret lives, cusped and crashing.
Know everything dazzles in the right light.

The Field That Resists Naming

You are taking a class in indifference.
You want to be able to ignore his hands

when they are not on your waist.
You carry your heart wrapped in waterproof cloth.

You can think of little else,
press yourself against walls.

You've been acutely aware
of nerve endings for weeks.

You are trying to be enough.

A bramble in his side.
A nightmoth.

The field that resists naming.

THE POND

Small places burst with love for you. My hand is an oar.
An eardrum expanding. A ribbon pulled across the wrist.
You hear bells ringing in another country, a sound
that echoes only in your head. Let me tell you how the bells
began to colonize even me. Let me tell you about the betrayal
of my organs. For the first time I knew why you wanted
out of this world. The way home was through your undoing.
For days you circled the pond, such a careful plotting.
I could only watch, finger the purple valance. And later,
I confess: I saw you walk into the pond, straight down
and into it, that terrible blue mouth. Who was I to prevent
your sinking, to call out, when nothing in this world deserved
you? Your floating hat gives you up, the housekeeper rushing
to pull you back. My reckless emissary, my drowning fox—
you come back to me muted and heavy.

All You Can Do Is Imagine the Leaving

He hasn't left yet but all you can do is imagine the leaving. You
are playing an old game and when he says there are no losers
he means "king me." You want to have your cake and eat it,
but you also want his cake. You want to have all the cake. You
think you can pinpoint the spoils, but decide against highway robbery.
Settle for crumbs in the bottom of a large bowl. You are a week,
six months, a year ago. Cut past the quick, the nervous need.
                    The problem of small, winged birds.

False Narrative

In the morning,
stale salt from the pool of my back.

For you, at the window, I dress
slowly, and the light.

We cure our deficiencies like this—
shivers erupting across the scalp.

As always when you leave: bare box.
A mockery.

Your absence a knock,
persistent and fractured.

And I'm rabid for anything, a grief system.
You an abstraction. You the constituent parts.

I want to believe in one or two true things,
the grain of the traveled hillside, how I am massive in my love.

How We Prepared for War

It was necessary to become cold. To forget the lives
we'd dreamed of. The days were taut and full of smoke.
Our pockets were mostly empty. We practiced crawling
through progressively smaller holes. Made quick work
of a tangled bandage. You served me poisoned, oily fish
until my mouth became a bell that only you could hear.
I came to crave the lovely pain—my strange want—
and ate the fish with gusto. Every day prepared us
for the next explosion. I lived as though
you moved the earth, its axis stilled when you entered a room.
The slow ravage of my gut surprised no one. When the war began
I would stand stupid and stunned, unconvinced the world
could throttle on beyond our pause, our meticulous training.

In the Company of a Blue Apparatus

The night is a pale stalk, inside-out place. Terror gradient. Our
natural grief habitat. Dear breastbone, false door behind which
the imagined life exists. A culling, we were chanceless. We dress
in the company of a blue apparatus. Be my new garment. Capable
of an undoing, my errant limbs. You pin snow to my coat. A flinch
surrounds us heavily. I turn on my slim, quick heel. Bleed where bees
can't. Still throwing stitches into the gash left. I will follow the slack
line to your mouth. Your cheekbone the measure of all soft curves.
Filaments expand till they shatter, made spectacular by ruin.

We will both be dead in five years.

II.

This Is a Life

For you every day was a war. There was never enough light.
The spot on your wrist was always turning into a bird
whose neck you'd broken. I walked around behind you,
picking up the dark feathers. I made you a crown,
lived on my knees for you. I was a ghost, the same
in each city where you weren't. This was a life we'd chosen.
The fields never looked the same once we walked them.

Definition Of

An animal comes back
to its nest to find the eggs destroyed.
A storm crosshatches the meadow.
Leaves, and silt through the canopy.
To come to you willingly—
even now I ask for this ache.

The Trick Is Small

I am less careful now when I speak to you
but too much faith is dangerous.

A word that isn't *comfort*
leaves me measuring in gestures.

The fissure of a quiet mouth.
I am liable to start filling

the spaces between words
but you tongue my eyelids closed.

I'll be accountable for that narrative.
That impure sprawl.

I put on my blue shirt
but everything is yellow.

HULL

It begins as a twinge between
the legs, creeping upward
into my chest before I can
name the hurt. When I learn
to name it: carnelian, telescope,
planchette. Cracked womb, split organ.
Crazed with love for a dead thing
expelled, my own red hull an empty
pouch. I could never be sure
of the walls around me, the soft words
of wallpaper, the frames that couldn't
hold your picture. Your face is a shape
behind my eyes, swell of honeyed
hair and citrine. Even in my grief I think
of the morning we shared a lime,
touched the pucker of the other's lips.
Another tragedy no one else could see.

ABSENCE ANATOMY

A whirring in the ear is not unwelcome.
Nor all these apples I've hollowed into mouths.

A heavy box seems sewn inside my chest
and no amount of thumping will unstick it.

You cut your hand and I wanted
to touch the exposed tendon,

to understand finally how hands move.
How my palm could be the shape of absence.

It's almost time to leave.

The thistle is ready to break open.
There might be something to salvage—

the dish filled with apricots, at least.

I wish I'd filled a drawer
with my most prized possessions.

Hair pin, hydrogen.
Heart scraped clean.

GRETE WRITES TO GEORG AT WAR

You've started to write
about black horses again,
dear, but I can only envy

the mouse with his quick,
imperfect heart. My own
is churlish, rimed, too slow.

I've been drifting, lately,
collecting bobbins since
you left. What you don't

know is that your going
was an ocean. The hollow
I could call *love*. I heard

you saw men dead in a field.

G, you might have been the prize.
The salt packed in my organs,
the magnificent shore.

I would give myself up
to your hands, finally
planchette, your silent, dear queen.

WHERE WE ARE BOTH WELL

Grant me soon the release for which I long.
—GRETE TRAKL, NOVEMBER 19, 1914

There is little to say now, and I am bitten,
pocked with your absence. Mostly I think

of your torso, invisible storm idling.
I imagine the room is a forest where we are both well.

A plate of oranges might sustain us for days.
I wake to find someone has replaced my heart.

My hands peel and blister, and I grieve for skin
you once touched. The house has begun to rot, swaths

of paper hanging from the walls, great pieces of the floor
gone soft. I will learn to walk again in a country

where you don't exist. I am a reluctant party to this undoing,
dazed and unmoored, the last tusked elephant in a forest of hunters.

Nocturne

I kept my music in a tower.
I was content to play for no one.

It's no longer delivered easily—
The keys hazed with powder.

The heft an uncommon voltage,
At once uncanny and amplified.

Escape or interlude,
And always the empty seats at the piano.

I took my leave of suffering.
My treason, my silver index.

On Never Marrying Him

We let it sit, heavy thing with thorns.
The table sags under limp stems.

We poke at it, continue this blue
dissection, brash microscoping.

I could tell you how it feels to hold
a dead thing, to be content

with rings of pollen instead of metal.
I want to lie and lie and tell you

I am the bad you need. Anything
you've ever been denied.

It doesn't have to mean,
the way glass catches the light.

And we are used to alone now,
the tender cartography of our bodies

moving on parallel streets. The worth
of our undoing, brightest blaze inside me.

On my knees for any handful of earth.

LITTLE PIECES

At night you imagine
the way he might hold

a piece of fruit
on his tongue,

pressing down—

the inevitable burst
before finally pulling it in.

You will fail
in the most spectacular

of ways, cling to the root
of this and the brash screech.

The lead veins of the window.

Here is the answer—
the cracked cuticle,

the broken binding.

The whole of the town
deforested and cleared of shade.

DREAM II

A woman in a yellow dress
          is disappearing down the hill
in front of you.

You are carrying an axe,
          which isn't misplaced.

Misdirection is a fun new game you're trying.

Each strand of your hair is hollow
          and expands when wet.

A large cat is circling around you;
          the tilt of its mouth means something sinister.

Nothing meant to last does,
          and waking its own danger.

A troubled feeling
          skulks through your day.

You want as much as you can take
          and then you want it doubled.

A new country for your longing.

Poem about Desire

The street outside my window
never darkens,

brash city for a girl made new,
girl cast in brass.

These rooms are enough.
Even the hallway: mine.

Some Elaborate

Brother, you began to leave me early,
chose to offer yourself to the ground
beneath horses and trains, refused
to focus on my face, this world
a water too murky to cleanly navigate

You leave me every day in small ways,
and I imagine your organs must be eroding,
your skin the only shoreline I want to visit,
and time a limit refused again and again

And I am bursting, my fist a hot planet,
my pelvis a meadow, and I will be the bell,
a war ending, our hearts some elaborate
pulley system, a line long enough
to stretch across countries

I am hostage to your absence,
filling a bucket, even the most familiar
street a wilderness I don't recognize,
a waterline I keep expecting will change

GIVEN THE DEPTH

To know this severing.
To be unwound in the service of your teeth.
To be wrecked by the hillside.
Anything that hurts more than a field.
What was found beneath a stone,
or the tenderness of any new skin.
For reference: this kind of luster.
All the world's loneliness stored in a vat.
We are afraid to want additional earth
given the depth of our wounds.
Residue of a fracturing,
milky tea gone cold.
Nothing is soothed.

Somewhere a Key

You are a sickness still lingering, rotten pit
to be rent from the chest, sour blood to drain.
Crows repeatedly fly into the windows.
Done numbing myself, or else the money's run out.
You must know I keep writing these letters,
missives dropped around the city, crumbs
for your ghost. Almost all the rooms inside me
are closed. Each time I write your name a key
somewhere turns in a lock.

III.

Spin

Word of your death comes on a Sunday,
your name there on the letter, *Trakl*,
in careful lettering. The city has begun
to unravel into dark filaments,
your name a rope drawn taut.
I discover your loss in new places:
a bruised plum, tender globe,
hoofprint filled with water.
Sound becomes pinched, each name
that isn't yours crumbling on my tongue.
Some nights you visit me in a dream,
your face pale and drawn. We speak
quietly and sit with our hands crossed.
You show me a bullet you've pulled
from another man's chest. It sits
on the table between us, heavy as though
it holds the whole war. Outside the window
men strap dead horses to the carousel.
They spin and spin and spin.

Grete Asks the Hard Question

I only exist in the word *sister*, spun through white fields
until I'm invisible to anyone who doesn't know I'm there.
I tell you my body is a hollow, a fence, how there are so many
colors I'll never see. Let me be refracted as you see best,
woman with blue eyebrows, the smallest deer. Is it wrong?
I know your heart is a cathedral. Sometimes you visit me
and your hands become birds, unfurl the whole forest.

ANIMUS

We meet on a bridge in the rain.
I know the perspective is wrong.
You are larger than the building.
Even from this angle.
We marry dressed in lilac.
Makes sense.
A hive of bees slated to die exists somewhere.
Through the glass it almost looks as if you love me.
A red fox runs under the overpass.
Your thigh fills most of the frame.
We became ferocious at sunset.
How many days will it last this time?
The orange chaise, and half-dressed.
You come up behind me with a whisper.
A red spool of string means our time is running out.
In the room you slip your finger between my breasts.
I have never touched you.
I would know it.

Keening

I am a gilded
horse, keening,

bent to the ground,

and I make those
terrible sounds

Dark morning,
I curse into the soil

the thought of it:

a hard, smooth stone

my voice a grenade
clever bomb

unearthed

If I could harden
my heart in the sun

I would crack
it in two, spin

the pieces like
dark red tops

POPPIES

You are far from home,
a body in a field I cannot visit.
Even my eyebrows: blue,
and split at the seams with your mention.

Give me only muted color,
black roses, a brown glass bottle.
Nothing that exists or dies loudly,
nothing you ever mentioned in a poem.

Because suddenly there are poppies everywhere,
thrust from the cracked streets,
and I want to rip their red heads
from the stems, powder the remains.

My body is a bruise, purpled with loss.
I am tired of swallowing your name,
finding ink on each of your shirts,
red petals in the pages of books.

MEN I COULD HAVE LOVED

You come to me like a growl.

Worship, the deer rising out of the river.

Mornings are an ending, the willing back

to sleep, the rowing toward the dream

just left. The day is lurid, and lingers

until something slips. Felt in the teeth.

What I would give to be the poppy or else

the black horse, veins laid out like a map

you'd just unfolded. The swelling of a pupil.

Most days it comes back, the brain trying to catch.

The space between our bodies a constellation

they haven't named yet.

LITANY FOR G

I have wanted all along to touch the bones
in your spine to rest my cheek against
the base of your neck I have wanted
to lie down in your place on the field I have
been poison and antidote I have bared my wrists
to you I have traced my fear on onionskin I have gathered
tin soldiers in a bowl I have been the clever keeper
of your heart I have touched your closed eye while
you slept the cool thin skin a surprise I have been replete
with lust I have watched from another room I have given
myself over to everything you've touched

Umwelt

we wake dry-mouthed and hang-tongued
        roll clumsily toward the brassy glow of hands
in the matchlight

all those bright, blossoming capillaries

veritable poison, our covetous hands
ether mouth

we silhouettes we relics

your dark gardens inviting me
        to ruin

you merrily drag your hem of bees
        till I sound you out

love a tantrum made palatable
only by its alternative

Wild Boat

Your presence demanded my tongue and so I made my body
an armory, took to lying under the floorboards. My heart became
a wild boat, in a storm in a haze in an hour, and its anchor grew
beneath me. I imagined it taking root on the seabed, twined
around a blind fish or scarred with kelp. It became harder
to leave the room and I stared at chipped tile to pass the time.
Your coat was strung on a line in the bathroom and so I couldn't
ignore it. It remained true that you died in a bed in Poland
and I hid from your death. It was worse than all the other facts.

IV.

Love Lustrum

1.

The ritual is over.
You have one less animal.

2.

Something gold
catches the eye.

3.

Lust folds in on you
like a paper bird.

4.

Bitter earthquake.

5.

You are no longer
interested in cages.

On the One-Year Anniversary of Your Death

I didn't wash for days after you died, stunk of you until he noticed,
until the smell became more painful than your absence. It wasn't ink,
or even a needle entering skin, just smoke, the way your palm
smells after holding something metal. The way I think of you now
is crystalline, fractured by necessity, light through a spidered window,
a copy of a copy of a copy. There are things you can no longer
read written on my face, his hands every night as I sleep, how his mouth
is a knife, breaking open the skin each time, and it dulls, it dulls, it dulls

To Coax a Wound

Went searching for you. Carrying what.
Portal, portent, and tightly bound. To coax
a wound. Waist mine, billowy whole of the thing.
O, to dissect a meander. To stalk a bulky feeling.
Bliss-flecked, and braiding the branches.
Couldn't track. Drug behind, peeling and singed.
Broken fence, I carouseled ruin. So devastating
in your shirtsleeves. No matter the sutures
in my chest, the sparkling eventuality. Safekeeping
heart poorly. Barely able to muster a cooing.

Poem about Desire

cheek bitten or
a wound named fury

yellow gust of hair

clear an outline in the brush
say you're bluffing, no, say

squall, say port, say anomaly

say the forest peeled itself back
its skin of bright branches

those veins broken open

close your hand around the wasp
as if allocated the sharp red sear

as if you can take it

SANATORIUM

My crown is slowly unfolding, here suddenly its hidden machinery
under all these lights. All the prickling trees seem willing
to take me on. I can no longer follow you through the crowd,
still trying to find a word for these burst nerves. This willingness
to sink. My atoms hurt, muscling their way into being. Everything
that's ever been said about constellations exists inside my chest.
The only consistent thing is felt in the haunches, an unwinding.
The days peel slowly and I can barely stand, spiraling surely
toward an alarming finale, fits lush as tumors,
such remarkable swellings. I would rupture if asked.

Burden and Roar

If bitten: an apple,   a stalk. Clumsy
          or maudlin and
the foreign taste of your wrist.
Perhaps I was a magpie,   a songbird.
Perhaps all burden and roar.
To tell you how   our bodies acted
while we slept. To give you my grain hands.
          My terrible heart.

Tethered

my grief gown my five-years-gone
my swamp mouth my obvious heart
my belly gnawed through
you inhabit the space beneath my fingernail
but you do not say you love my nail bed you
do not say it we trade the sorrow pack
across the table toothed & tethered
a localized numbness in my palm hard
to believe there might be an hour
not crowded with your incarnations might
be another hand at the small in my hair around
my neck might learn again to be desired

PARADISE

Brightly colored packages lined   up in a glass case
The feeling of a body   as it crests
The seeds of your favorite   invasive plant
Shuttering ferns, all the bruised   fruit
The wall   he pressed you against
Poison, just   in case
There are a hundred things   you want,
not just the steady   burn   near your sternum
A world in which you've never   been touched
An unnavigable garden
Each morning you are split   open again:
you want   the whole world
You might never   be satisfied

RIOT

Weather crowds
the city and I cling
to the walls.
The room is dark.

The rabbit in the yard
suddenly, miraculously still.

I am not afraid of any edge,
or stippled trail.
Or you, pocketheart.
        Splaying the line.

The table strewn
with blackberries.
The shades drawn,
the dearest sound.

Unfetter

Keep your body in limbo for weeks,
       somewhere between spoiling and hatching.

Hold it there, feel it feel it feel it—
       resurrection when you let it go.

Catch the terrible feelings in mason jars,
       tuck them deep into cupboards.

This is how you live without them.
       This is how you translate the wound.

Remember what it's like to trace letters
       on the mirror, to mark steamed glass

with any word. Tomorrow there will be fresh grass
       and you won't be afraid to adore it.

What Comes After

I sun myself under you, perfect the swagger. The slick length
of desire, and ours the darkest microscope. I wanted it striking,
sly, your hand on the bedpost. Projection, petri dish, sliver of sky.
When our need overwhelmed us, he became the easiest channel,
glass bridge between countries. I knew it quickly: the patterns
of his coat a poor substitute. Ecstasy was fickle, found in powders,
in holding my breath too long. After everything,
you were the only thing left on my heart. In the world
we were meant for: the ghost of our loss and what comes after.

The Poem about Birds I Can't Write

Look: here is the room
I want to fill with birds.

Window-walled and
humming; ripe with flight.

Swift, finch, hummingbird.
A buzzing released in my throat.

I imagine myself whole
in the center—

light streaming through glass,
streaked onto palms.

I tell you: wing against wing.
The unrealized, the impractical.

The way feathers glint in the
vines. Those old brambles.

How I jaw against the day
and you brace and brace.

Still, I lift myself toward
ruddy sky, crush your
faltering under my boot.

Dream myself laughing:
open-mouthed and
trembling in the aviary.

To G, after the Party

It's been a long night, the kind you crash out of.
Without you I've walked up and down the hall and none
of the doors are in the right place. I'm wearing the green dress
you liked best. I only see you in black horses, now,
blowing and pawing on street corners, in the cool metal
that, held, thrills my thigh. I wrote what I wanted most
on a bit of paper, rolled it in the mouth of the pistol
so the whole world would know it. Three years later
the party is over, and I am just a girl arriving late.
The lamps are turning off in all of the windows. I wonder
what it would have felt like to have a choice, to choose love,
to hold anything with both hands. It's taken me this long
to say *I want I want I want*, to take up the gun—to join you—

Living Without

We wake up on trains moving in opposite directions.
Find wires stretched like webs between trees.

The passenger pigeon gone since 1914.
His back curving into the bed.

How we would hear our muscles moving
if our ears were tuned to a lower frequency.

Notes

Epigraph (page ii) from Deborah Keenan, "Travel," *Willow Room, Green Door* (Minneapolis: Milkweed Editions, 2007).

"Whoever Drinks from Me"

This poem is loosely based on, and its epigraph taken from, D. L. Ashliman's translation of Jacob and Wilhelm Grimm, "Little Brother and Little Sister," http://www.pitt.edu/~dash/grimm011.html.

"Where We Are Both Well"

Epigraph from Grete Trakl, *Georg Trakl: A Profile*, ed. Frank Graziano (Durango, CO: Logbridge-Rhodes, 1983).

Works Consulted

Chiu, Ch. S., and Edith Borchardt. *Women in the Shadows: Mileva Einstein-Marić, Margarete Jeanne Trakl, Lise Meitner, Milena Jesenská, and Margarete Schütte-Lihotzky.* New York: Peter Lang, 2008.

Lindenberger, Herbert. *Georg Trakl.* New York: Twayne, 1971.

Trakl, Georg, and Frank Graziano. *Georg Trakl: A Profile.* Durango, CO: Logbridge-Rhodes, 1983.

Trakl, Georg, and Margitt Lehbert. *The Poems of Georg Trakl.* London: Anvil Press Poetry, 2007.

Trakl, Georg, and Stephen Tapscott. *Georg Trakl: Poems.* Oberlin, OH: Oberlin College Press, 2011.

"Wild Heart Turning White: Georg Trakl and Cocaine." *The Public Domain Review.* https://publicdomainreview. org/2014/10/29/wild-heart-turning-white-georg-trakl-and-cocaine/.

Acknowledgments

Many thanks to the editors of the following publications where some of these poems first appeared, sometimes in different forms:

Bateau: "All You Can Do Is Imagine the Leaving"

Carolina Quarterly: "Grete Asks the Hard Question," "This Is the House"

Carolina Quarterly Online: "Right Light"

Hayden's Ferry Review: "The Pond," "How We Prepared for War," "Spin"

Midway Journal: "Incantare," "On Never Marrying Him," "Some Elaborate"

Poetry City, USA: "Wild Boat," "Little Pieces"

Prairie Schooner: "Grete Writes to Georg at War"

Sugar House Review: "Detonate"

I'm enormously grateful to the Lindquist & Vennum Foundation for their generous support of poetry in the Midwest, to Srikanth Reddy for selecting this book, and to Daniel Slager, Joanna R. Demkiewicz, Joey McGarvey, Annie Harvieux, Mary Austin Speaker, and everyone at Milkweed Editions.

Endless thanks to Deborah Keenan, Katrina Vandenberg, Jim Moore, Patricia Kirkpatrick, Ryo Yamaguchi, Patricia Smith, Peter Campion, Mike Main, Kevin Lally, Elena Cisneros, Jenny McDougal, Paige Riehl, Lauren Heavey, Rick Cedergren, Kevin Morrison, Welcome Jerde, Pam Schmid, Kristin Fitzsimmons, Isadora Gruye, Ember Johnson, Steven Lang, Sandra Evans, Elizabeth DiGrazia, Toni Halleen, Maureen Fischer, Vanessa Ramos, Samantha Silker, and Jacob and Rebecca Wanous.

Thanks, especially, to: my brilliant sisters—Kelsey, Arianna, and Meerah; my Mother, for her unflinching, enormous love; my Father, for his wisdom and support; my dear family; Sarah Cedergren, Emily Kolbinger, and Gretchen Marquette for loving me so well; and Matt, for bravery and laughter.

Lucas Botz

CAITLIN BAILEY has published poems in *Prairie Schooner,* *Hayden's Ferry Review,* *Carolina Quarterly,* and elsewhere. She received her MFA from Hamline University and lives in Saint Paul, Minnesota.

The sixth award of

THE LINDQUIST & VENNUM PRIZE FOR POETRY

is presented to

CAITLIN BAILEY

by

MILKWEED EDITIONS
and
THE LINDQUIST & VENNUM FOUNDATION

Established in 2011, the annual Lindquist & Vennum Prize for Poetry awards $10,000 and publication by Milkweed Editions to a poet residing in North Dakota, South Dakota, Minnesota, Iowa, or Wisconsin. Finalists are selected from among all entrants by the editors of Milkweed Editions. The winning collection is selected annually by an independent judge. The 2017 Lindquist & Vennum Prize for Poetry was judged by Srikanth Reddy.

Milkweed Editions is one of the nation's leading independent publishers. We believe that literature has the potential to change the way we see the world, and that bringing new voices to essential conversations is the clearest path to ensuring a vibrant, diverse, and empowered future. The Lindquist & Vennum Foundation was established by the Minneapolis-headquartered law firm of Lindquist & Vennum, LLP, and is a donor-advised fund of The Minneapolis Foundation.

Founded as a nonprofit organization in 1980, Milkweed Editions is an independent publisher. Our mission is to identify, nurture and publish transformative literature, and build an engaged community around it.

milkweed.org

Interior design and typesetting by Mary Austin Speaker
Typeset in Adobe Jenson

Adobe Jenson was designed by Robert Slimbach for Adobe and released in 1996. Slimbach based Jenson's roman styles on a text face cut by fifteenth-century type designer Nicolas Jenson, and its italics are based on type created by Ludovico Vicentino degli Arrighi, a late fifteenth-century papal scribe and type designer.